Dominie
Marine Life

Sea Snakes

Contents

Text by Stanley L. Swartz
Photography by Robert Yin

🔾 Dominie Press, Inc.

About Sea Snakes

There are more than fifty **species** of sea snakes. Sea snakes are reptiles. They live in **tropical** waters.

◀ Banded Sea Krait

How Sea Snakes Breathe

Sea snakes breathe air, just like other snakes. They have a large lung, which they use for breathing. They can stay under water for more than two hours.

◀ Banded Sea Krait

Sea snakes' nostrils have flaps. These flaps close when they go under water. The closed flaps stop the intake of salt water.

◄ Turtlehead Sea Snake

How They Drink Salt Water

Sea snakes have special glands in their mouths. These glands remove salt from the water and **excrete** it from the sea snakes. This allows sea snakes to drink salt water.

◀ **Banded Sea Krait Head**

Their Venom

All sea snakes are **poisonous**. Their **venom** is much more **toxic** than that of a cobra. However, sea snakes do not inject as much poison into their **prey**.

◄ Turtlehead Sea Snake

How They Survive

Sea snakes **survive** on a **diet** of fish, fish eggs, and eels. Most sea snakes give birth at sea. A few lay their eggs on shore.

◄ **Banded Sea Krait**

Their Skins

Sea snakes are not very large.
They grow to be 1½ to 3½ feet long.
They **shed** their outer skin about
every two weeks.

◄ Banded Sea Krait

Sea snakes have scales on their skin. They also have a flattened tail. This makes them good swimmers and divers.

◄ Sea Snake Skin

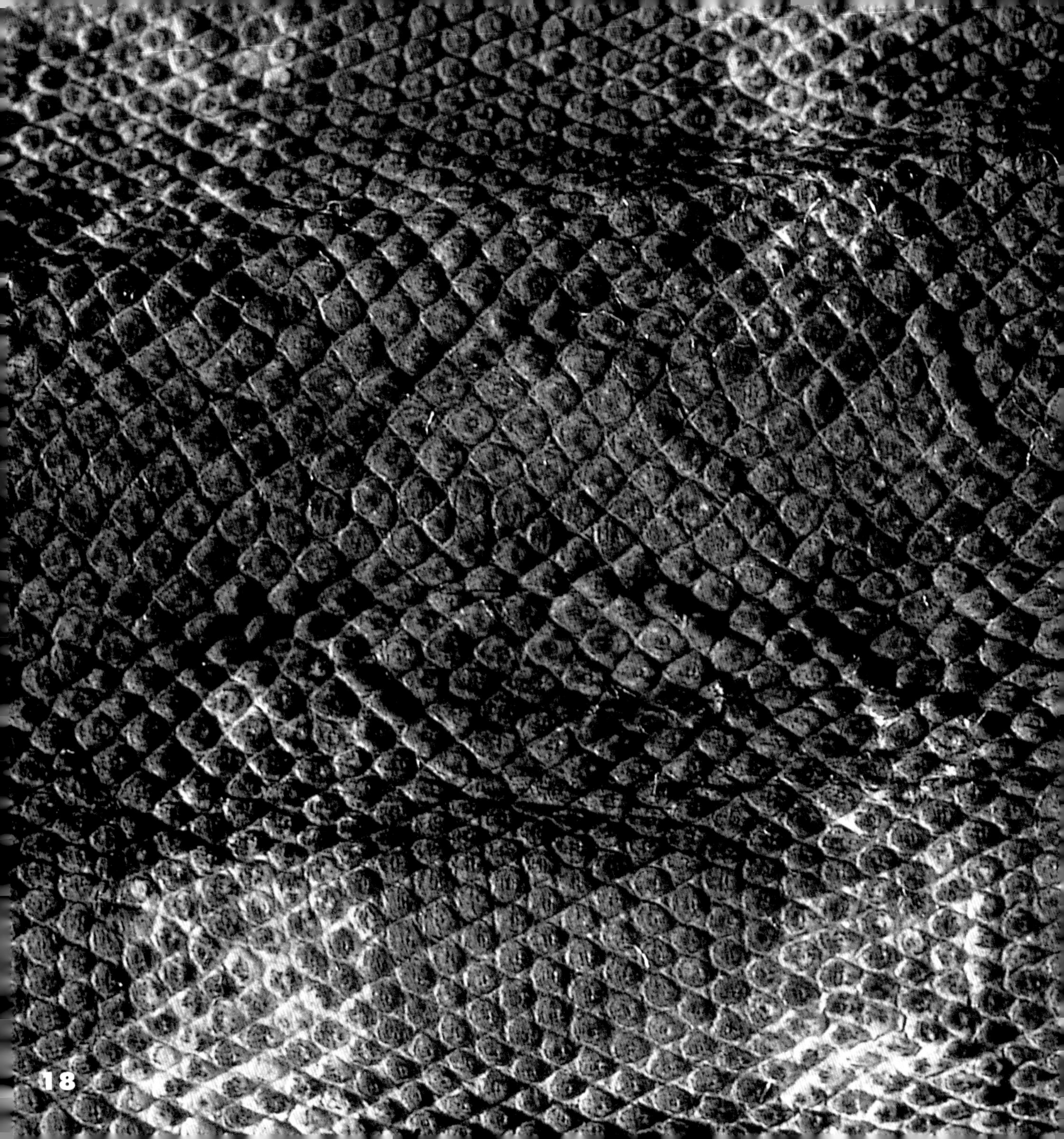

Sea snakes are **prized** for their skins. The skins are first dried. Some are **dyed** to make things with beautiful colors.

◄ **Sea Snake Skin**

Many things can be made from sea snake skins. The skin in this photograph was dyed. Then it was used to make this pair of shoes.

◀ **Woman with Shoes Made from Sea Snake Skin**

Purses are also made from sea snake skins that have been shed. Even jewelry and hair ornaments are made from sea snake skins. Look at the many colors in these items.

◄ **Jewelry Made from Sea Snake Skin**

Glossary

diet:	The food that an animal or a person usually eats
dyed:	Colored by a special liquid
excrete:	To get rid of something that is not needed or wanted
poisonous:	Able to cause illness or death
prey:	Animals that are hunted and eaten by other animals
prized:	Highly valued
shed:	To lose; to get rid of
species:	Types of animals that have some physical characteristics in common
survive:	To stay alive
toxic:	Poisonous; deadly
tropical:	Areas of land or water that are very warm throughout the year
venom:	Deadly poison

Index